HINDU
BABY NAMES
FOR BOYS AND GIRLS

Compiled by :
SANGEETA VARMA

HINDU
Baby Names
2100 BEAUTIFUL NAMES FOR BOYS AND GIRLS

हिन्दु
बच्चों के नाम
बच्चों के लिए 2100 सुन्दर एवं सार्थक नाम

Compiled by :
SANGEETA VARMA

© Star Publications

ISBN : 978-81-7650-328-0

HINDU BABY NAMES
Sangeeta Varma (Comp.)

Revised Enlarged Edition : 2008
Price : Rs. 99.00 (£ 4.95)

Published by :
Star Publications (P) Ltd.
4/5, Asaf Ali Road, New Delhi-110002 (INDIA)
Phone : 091-23257220
E-mail : starpub@satyam.net.in

Type setted by Wasi Prints, Delhi.
Printed at Lahooti Offset Press, Delhi

BIRTH-DATES AND BIRTH-SIGNS :

In modern times birth *signs of both boys and girls are based upon their dates of birth, whereas in ancient Indian astrology, first alphabet of the name was related to the sign of birth. Both these systems are considered to be equally accurate, and it is one's belief which makes him/her to decide about birth sign.*

We are giving below all the 12 birth signs with their relevance to birth dates, as also to the first Hindi alphabet of the name :

Birth Sign	राशि	First Hindi Alphabet of name :	Date of Birth (as per English Calender)
ARIES	मेष	चू चे चो ला ली लू ले लो आ	21 Mar. — 20 Apr.
TAURUS	वृष	ई उ ए ओ वा वी वू वे वो	21 Apr. — 20 May.
GEMINI	मिथुन	का की कू घ ड छ के को हा	21 May. — 21 June.
CANCER	कर्क	ही हू हे ही डा डी डू डे डो	22 June. — 22 July.
LEO	सिंह	मामी मू मे मो टा टी टू टे	23 July. — 23 Aug.
VIRGO	कन्या	टो पा पी पू श ण ठ पे पो	24 Aug. — 23 Sep.
LIBRA	तुला	रा री रू रे रो ता ती तू ते	24 Sep. — 23 Oct.
SCORPIO	वृश्चिक	तोना नी नू नो या यी यू	24 Oct. — 22 Nov. .
SAGITTAROUS	धनु	ये यो भा भी भू धा फा ढा भे	23 Nov. — 21 Dec.
CAPRICORN	मकर	भो जा जी खी खे खो गा गी	22 Dec. — 20 Jan.
AQUARIUS	कुंभ	गू गे गो सा सी सू से सो दा	21 Jan. — 18 Feb.
PISCES	मीन	दी दू थ झ त्र दे दो चा ची	19 Feb. — 20 Mar.

PREFACE

Shakespeare had once written : "rose is a rose is a rose, whatever name it may have." It is not true and I differ with this saying. In my opinion, the word "rose" has its own fragrance.

This is more so while naming a child. In any community and religion, naming of a child is very important and special celebrations are held on such occasion.

This book is a presentation to suggest popular and meaningful names for both boys and girls in Hindu families.

There was a time when names of Gods and Goddesses were very popular, and most of the names were related to such religious deities. Such names are still popular, because as long as Hindu community is alive, there will always be names like Rama, Krishan, Hari, Govind, Radha, Lakshmi, Saraswati etc. However, modern trend has introduced a more comprehensive listing of such names. Especially in urban communities, short and simple names are more popular, like Anil, Meera, Nisha, Sangeeta etc. Similarly, names with some specific meanings are much of the liking, even if they are from Sanskrit or from our mythology.

In the modern times, many names are equally suitable for a boy and a girl, like Santosh (सन्तोष) meaning satisfaction, is a common name for both boys and girls.

This collection of over 2100 Hindu names has been compliled with the purpose to suggest meaningful, simple and impressive names for both genders. Many of the names are suitable for both boys and girls equally just by making certain variations, like adding or deleting 'a' at the end of the word. Most of the names in this book are based on religious and mythological characters, which may or may not have any dictionary meanings.

Some of the names in this book can be written or read in more than one way, e.g. 'Alkaa' or 'Chaaru' can be written as 'Alka' or 'Charu' more correctly. This has been done only to emphasise the right pronunciation.

There are many books available on this subject in the market today, but this is a unique publication. Firstly, this book has been compiled in Roman script; and secondly, each name has been given in both Hindi and Roman script, with meanings or reference of the word in English, which will make it useful for even non-Hindi speaking world. This book will be of great interest among Hindus settled abroad, where chosing suitable and meaningful names for Hindu children is not so difficult.

This is a book which every person would like to posses, not only for his or her own child, but also for all friends and relatives who will feel greatly obliged if a copy of this book is presented to them.

—**Compiler**

A   अ, आ

Aabha	आभा	light, splendour
Aabheer	आभीर	a cow herd
Adarsh	आदर्श	ideal
Aadidev	आदिदेव	the first god
Aadinath	आदिनाथ	the first god
Aditya	आदित्य	the sun
Aagam	आगम	coming/ arrival
Aagney	आग्नेय	son of the fire
Aahlad	आह्लाद	delight
Aahlaadita	आहलादिता	in a happy mood
Akaash	आकाश	sky
Akanksha	आकांक्षा	desire
Aalok	आलोक	lustre
Aaloka	आलोका	lustrous
Aamod	आमोद	pleasant
Amra-Pali	आम्रपाली	leaf of mango tree
Anand Swarup	आनन्द स्वरूप	full of joy
Anand	आनन्द	joy
Anandamayi	आनन्दमयी	very happy
Anandi	आनन्दी	always happy (woman)
Anandita	आनन्दिता	very happy
Anjaney	आंजनेय	name of Hanuman
Aapt	आप्त	trust worthy
Aapti	आप्ति	fulfillment

Araadhak	आराधक	worshipper
Aarati	आरती	prayer
Aarushi	आरुषि	daughter of Manu
Aasha	आशा	hope
Aasha-Lata	आशा-लता	creeper of hope
Aashish	आशीष	blessing
Aashlesh	आश्लेष	to embrace
Ashutosh	आशुतोष	who is easily pleased
Aastik	आस्तिक	who has faith in god
Atmaj	आत्मज	son
Aatrey	आत्रेय	an ancient mythological name
Ayu	आयु	span of life
Ayushmaan	आयुष्मान	long life
Abhay	अभय	free from fear
Abhibhav	अभिभव	victorious
Abhijaat	अभिजात	well-borne
Abhijaata	अभिजाता	well borne (woman)
Abhijay	अभिजय	victorious
Abhijit	अभिजित	victorious
Abhijita	अभिजिता	victorious (woman)
Abhimaani	अभिमानी	who possess self respect
Abhimanyu	अभिमन्यु	son of Arjuna
Abhinav	अभिनव	brand new
Abhinay	अभिनय	performance
Abhiraam	अभिराम	pleasing
Abhirath	अभिरथ	great chariotes

Abhirup	अभिरूप	handsome
Abhirupa	अभिरूपा	beautiful (woman)
Abhisarika	अभिसारिका	a beloved
Abhishek	अभिषेक	to sprinkle, royal ceremony
Abhivaadan	अभिवादन	salute
Achal	अचल	unmoving
Achala	अचला	the earth
Achalendra	अचलेन्द्र	the Himalayas
Achintya	अचिन्त्य	beyond thought
Achira	अचिरा	very short
Achyut	अच्युत	indestructible
Adheer	अधीर	restless
Adheesh	अधीष्ठा	King
Adhip	अधिप	King
Aditi	अदिति	infinite
Agastya	अगस्त्य	name of a saint
Agnimitra	अग्निमित्र	friend of fire
Agnivesh	अग्निवेष	an ancient mythological name
Agyey	अज्ञेय	unknown
Ahilya	अहिल्या	a famous historical name
Airaawat	ऐरावत	the clestial elephant
Aishwarya	ऐश्वर्य	prosperity
Aj	अज	not born
Aja	अजा	shakti
Ajamil	अजामिल	unfriendly

Ajat	अजात	unborn
Ajatshatru	अजातशत्रु	who has no enemies
Ajay	अजय	unconquerable
Ajit	अजित	unconquerable
Ajitabh	अजिताभ	whose lustre can't be diminished
Ajitesh	अजितेश	victorious God
Akhil	अखिल	entire
Akhilesh	अखिलेश	lord of universe
Akhshi	अक्षी	eye, the pupil
Akrur	अक्रूर	simple, polite
Akshat	अक्षत	uninjured, intact
Akshay Keerti	अक्षयकीर्ति	eternal fame
Akshay	अक्षय	immortal
Akul	अकुल	rootless Shiva
Alak	अलक	lock of curly hair
Alaka	अलका	capital of Kuber dynasty (woman)
Alakananda	अलकनन्दा	name of a river
Alop	अलोप	who does not disappear
Alpana	अल्पना	decoration
Amala	अमला	pure
Amalendu	अमलेन्दु	full moon
Amaresh	अमरेश	name of Lord Indra
Amarnath	अमरनाथ	immortal lord
Amba	अम्बा	mother

Ambalika	अंबालिका	mother
Ambar	अंबर	sky
Ambareesh	अंबरीश	name of ancient king
Ambika	अंबिका	goddess Durga
Ambuja	अंबुजा	lotus
Ameet	अमीत	boundless
Amey	अमेय	boundless
Amit	अमित	boundless
Amitaabh	अमिताभ	boundless lustre
Amitesh	अमितेश	infinite god
Amiya	अमिय	nector
Amogh	अमोघ	unerring
Amol	अमोल	valuable
Amoolya	अमूल्य	precious
Amrit	अमृत	nectar
Amrita	अमृता	nector (woman)
Amurat	अमूर्त	formless
Anaadi	अनादि	without beginning
Anagh	अनघ	sinless
Anamika	अनामिका	fourth finger, namelss
Anand	आनन्द	pleasure
Anang	अनंग	cupid
Anangi	अनंगी	sexy
Anant	अनन्त	infinite
Ananta	अनन्ता	eternal (woman)

Ananya	अनन्या	incomparable
Anek	अनेक	many
Aneshwar	अनेश्वर	eternal
Angad	अंगद	an ornament
Angaja	अंगजा	daughter
Angira	अंगिरा	mother of Brahaspati
Aniket	अनिकेत	homeless
Anil	अनिल	god of wind
Anilaabh	अनिलाभ	zephyr
Anima	अणिमा	the power of becoming small
Animesh	अनिमेश	who does not wink
Aniruddh	अनिरुद्ध	which cannot be restricted
Anjali	अंजली	homage
Anjana	अंजना	mother of Hanuman
Annada	अन्नदा	goddess of food
Annapurna	अन्नपूर्णा	goddess of food
Anoop	अनूप	unequalled
Anshu	अंशु	ray of the sun
Anshuk	अंशुक	radiant
Anshumaala	अंशुमाला	garland of rays
Anshuman	अंशुमन	the sun
Antariksh	अंतरिक्ष	space
Anu	अनु	a prefix, atom
Anubhuti	अनुभूति	experience
Anuj	अनुज	younger brother

Anuloma	अनुलोमा	sequence
Anupama	अनुपमा	incomparable
Anupriya	अनुप्रिया	incomparable
Anuraadha	अनुराधा	one of the stars
Anuraag	अनुराग	love
Anuttara	अनुत्तरा	unanswerable
Anvita	अन्विता	who bridges the gap (woman)
Apara	अपरा	boundless, divine
Aparaajita	अपराजिता	unconquerable (woman)
Aparna	अपर्णा	leaf less
Aparoopa	अपरूपा	extremely beautiful
Apeksha	अपेक्षा	expectation
Apoorv	अपूर्व	quite new
Aranav	अर्णव	ocean
Archana	अर्चना	prayer
Archit	अर्चित	worshipped
Archita	अर्चिता	worshipped (woman)
Arhat	अर्हत	respectable
Arihant	अरिहन्त	killer of enemies
Arjun	अर्जुन	one of the Pandava brothers
Arpita	अर्पिता	which is offered, dedicated
Arun	अरुण	the dawn
Arundhati	अरुन्धती	the morning star
Arunima	अरुणिमा	reddishness

Arvind	अरविंद	a lotus
Arya	आर्य	noble
Aryama	अर्यमा	the sun
Ashesh	अशेष	entire
Ashok	अशोक	without sorrow, an eminent King
Ashwaghosh	अश्वघोज़	name of Buddhist philosopher
Ashwatthama	अश्वत्थामा	son of Dronacharya
Ashwini	अश्विनी	female horse, one of the stars
Asit	असित	not white, dark
Asit-varan	असितवरण	dark complexioned
Asmita	अस्मिता	who has ego
Atithi	अतिथि	guest
Atrey	अत्रेय	name of a saint
Atul	अतुल	unparalleled
Atulya	अतुल्य	unequalled (woman)
Avalok	अवलोक	who beholds
Avaneesh	अवनीश	master of the earth
Avani	अवनि	the earth
Avanindra	अवनिन्द्र	King of the earth
Avanti	अवन्ति	name of a historical city
Avantika	अवन्तिका	a city
Avtaar	अवतार	incarnation

B ब, भ

Bankim	बंकिम	not straight
Baadal	बादल	cloud
Bageshwari	बागेश्वरी	goddess of speech
Bala	बाला	young girl
Bhramar	भ्रमर	black bee
Ball-Krishan	बालकृष्ण	young Krishna
Baalark	बालार्क	the rising sun
Baanbhatt	बाणभट्ट	name of an ancient poet
Banke Bihari	बांके बिहारी	name of Krishna
Badri	बद्री	a sacred Hindu pilgrim
Bahupriya	बहुप्रिया	dear to all
Bahudhan	बहुधन	wealthy
Bakul	बकुल	a kind of tree
Bakula	बकुला	a kind of flower (woman)
Bali	बली	brave
Balbhadra	बलभद्र	strong and good, brother of Krishna
Balkrishna	बालकृष्ण	child Krishna
Balvant	बलवन्त	of immense strong
Bansi	बंशी	flute
Bansidhar	बंशीधर	man with a flute, Krishna
Batuk	बटूक	a religious man

Bela	बेला	time, a plant
Bhagya	भाग्य	fate, luck
Bhagyalakshmi	भाग्यलक्ष्मी	goddess of prosperity
Bhaama	भामा	passionate
Bhaamini	भामिनी	beautiful woman
Bhalendra	भालेन्द्र	lord of light
Bhamah	भामह	the sun
Bhanu	भानु	sun
Bhanuja	भानुजा	name of river Yamuna
Bhanumati	भानुमती	beautiful woman
Bhanupriya	भानुप्रिया	loved by the sun
Bhaavan	भावन	like-able
Bhaavana	भावना	feeling
Bharat	भरत	brother of Lord Rama
Bhaarat	भारत	India, son of Shakuntala
Bhaskar	भास्कर	the sun
Bhasvan	भास्वन	bright
Bhaswar	भास्वर	shining
Bhaswati	भास्वती	luminous
Bharati	भारती	the goddess of speech
Bhavini	भाविनी	beautiful woman
Bhagirath	भगीरथ	name of an ancient King
Bhagirathi	भागीरथी	name of Ganges river(woman)
Bhadra	भद्रा	gentle woman
Bhav-bhooti	भवभूति	the universe

Bhagavati	भगवती	goddess Parvati, fortunes
Bhairavi	भैरवी	goddess Kali
Bhakti	भक्ति	devotion
Bhagvaan	भगवान	the lord
Bhartrihari	भर्तृहरि	name of a celebrated poet
Bhaumik	भौमिक	lord of earth
Bhavani	भवानी	name of goddess Parvati
Bhavesh	भवश	lord of the world
Bhavya	भव्य	splendorous
Bhavya	भव्या	splendorous (woman)
Bheema	भीम	stronge (woman)
Bheem	भीम	dreadful, brave
Bheemsen	भीमसेन	son of brave man
Bheesham	भीष्म	a character of Mahabharata, strong
Bhoj	भोज	meal, name of a king
Bhrigu	भृगु	name of a saint
Bhoomi	भूमि	the earth
Bhoomija	भूमिजा	earth-born, another name of Sita
Bhoopendra	भूपेन्द्र	king of the earth
Bhoopat	भूपत	lord of the earth
Bhushan	भूषण	ornaments
Bhuvan	भुवन	the world
Bhuvanesh	भुवनेश	lord of the world
Bhuvaneshwar	भुवनेश्वर	lord of the world
Bhuvaneshwari	भुवनेश्वरी	goddess of earth (woman)

Bimbisaar	बिम्बिसार	king of Gupta dynasty
Bindiya	बिंदिया	a droplet
Bindu	बिंदु	a drop, dot
Bindusar	बिन्दुसर	an eminent King
Bindumalini	बिंदुमालिनी	who wears garland of pearls
Bindumati	बिंदुमती	queen
Biraaj	बिराज	shining
Birendra	बीरेन्द्र	warrior
Bipin	बिपिन	forest
Brahma	ब्रह्मा	supreme being, creater of human beings
Brahmaanand	ब्रह्मानन्द	supreme joy,
Brahmdev	ब्रह्मदेव	Lord Brahma
Brahmrishi	ब्रह्मऋषि	saint
Brja	ब्रज	place where lord Krishna was brought up
Brajamohan	ब्रजमोहन	name of lord Krishna
Brajesh	ब्रजेष	lord of Braj land
Brajendra	ब्रजेन्द्र	lord of Braj land
Brajraj	ब्रजराज	King of Braj land
Buddh	बुद्ध	awakened, lord Buddha
Buddhi	बुद्धि	intelligence
Buddhijivi	बुद्धिजीवी	intelligent

C च, छा

Cahndravati	चन्द्रावती	illuminated by moon
Chamundeshwari	चामुंडेश्वरी	goddess Durga
Chamundi	चामुंडी	goddess durga
Chanakya	चाणक्य	name of Kautilya, an ancient economist
Chaand	चांद	moon
Chaandani	चांदनी	moon light
Charu	चारु	beautiful
Charubaala	चारुबाला	beautiful girl
Charu-chanandra	चारुचन्द्र	beautiful moon
Charudatt	चारुदत्त	born of beauty
Charuhaas	चारुहास	with beautiful smile
Charuhasini	चारुहासिनी	beautiful smiling lady
Chahna	चाहना	affection
Chaitaali	चैताली	born in Hindu month of chaitra
Chaitanya	चैतन्य	sansitive, alert
Chaitra	चैत्र	Hindu calender month
Chaitri	चैत्री	born in Hindu month chaitra (woman)
Chaitya	चैत्य	place of worship
Chakor	चकोर	a bird
Chakradhar	चक्रधर	name of lord Vishnu

Chakrapani	चक्रपाणि	name of lord Vishnu
Chakravarti	चक्रवर्ती	a sovereign king
Chakresh	चक्रेश	name of lord Vishnu
Chakshu	चक्षु	eye
Chakshumati	चक्षुमती	lady with beautiful eyes
Chaman	चमन	garden
Chameli	चमेली	jasmine flower
Champa	चम्पा	fragrant flower
Champavati	चंपावती	lady with ornaments
Champak	चम्पक	a flower
Champa-Kali	चंपाकली	an ornament
Champika	चंपिका	name of Kush's wife
Chanak	चणक	father of Chanakya
Chanchal	चंचल	impatient
Chanchala	चंचला	impatient, lively (woman)
Chanchareek	चंचरीक	bee
Chanda	चंदा	moon (female)
Chandaalika	चंडालिका	name of goddess Durgaa
Chandan	चंदन	sandalwood
Chandavarman	चंडवर्मन	an old King
Chandeedaas	चंडीदास	name of a saint
Chandi	चंडी	goddess Durga
Chandi	चांदी	silver
Chandika	चंडिका	name of goddess Durga
Chandra Kiran	चन्द्रकिरन	moon beam

Chandra Kirti	चन्द्रकीर्ति	prestigious like moon
Chandra	चन्द्र	moon
Chandrabha	चन्द्राभा	lustre of moon light
Chandraditya	चंद्रादित्य	name of an ancient King
Chandrali	चन्द्राली	moonbeam
Chandranan	चन्द्रानन	moon-like face
Chandrani	चन्द्राणी	wife of moon
Chandravali	चन्द्रावली	a friend of Radha (woman)
Chandrayan	चन्द्रायण	the moon
Chandrabhaanu	चन्द्रभानु	ray of moon
Chandrachood	चन्द्रचूड़	name of lord Shiva
Chandragupt	चन्द्रगुप्त	name of an ancient king
Chandrahaas	चन्द्रहास	smiling like a moon
Chandrajyoti	चन्द्रज्योति	moonlight
Chandrakanta	चन्द्रकान्ता	night, lustre of moonlight
Chandrakala	चन्द्रकला	beauty of moon
Chandrakeerti	चन्द्रकीर्ति	glory of moon
Chandraketu	चन्द्रकेतु	moon banner, son of Lakshman
Chandralekha	चन्द्रलेखा	digit of the moon
Chandrama	चन्द्रमा	the moon
Chandramadhav	चन्द्रमाधव	sweet
Chandramaala	चन्द्रमाला	a garland of moon
Chandramasi	चन्द्रमासी	wife of Brihaspati
Chandramallika	चन्द्रमल्लिका	jasmine

Chandramani	चन्द्रमणि	moon stone
Chandramauli	चन्द्रमौलि	name of Shiva, crest jewel
Chandramukhi	चन्द्रमुखी	moonfaced
Chandra-Peed	चन्द्रापीड	name of Shiva
Chandraprabha	चन्द्रप्रभा	lustre of the moon
Chandraprakash	चन्द्रप्रकाश	moon light
Chandra-rekha	चन्द्ररेखा	streak of the moon
Chandrashekhar	चन्द्रशेखर	name of Shiva
Chandravadan	चन्द्रवदन	moon-like face
Chandravadana	चन्द्रवदना	moon-like face (female)
Chandravadani	चन्द्रवदनी	moon-like face (female)
Chandresh	चन्द्रेश	King of the moon
Chandrika	चन्द्रिका	moon light
Chandrima	चन्द्रिमा	the moon
Chapal	चपल	unsteady, clever
Chapala	चपला	clever (female)
Charak	चरक	an ancient physician
Charan	चरण	feet
Charchika	चर्चिका	a goddess
Charuchitra	चारुचित्र	beautiful picture (woman)
Charukeshi	चारुकेशी	with beautiful hair (woman)
Charulata	चारुलता	beautiful creeper (woman)
Charumati	चारुमती	endowed with beauty (woman)
Charunetra	चारुनेत्रा	with beautiful eyes (woman)

Charusheel	चारुशील	of good character
Charusheela	चारुशीला	of good character (female)
Charuvrat	चारुव्रत	of good character
Charuvrata	चारुव्रता	good character (female)
Charvangi	चार्वंगी	with beautiful body
Charvi	चार्वी	beloved
Chatur	चतुर	clever
Chaturaanan	चतुरानन	with four eyes
Chaturbhuj	चतुर्भुज	with four arms
Cheshta	चेष्टा	desire
Chetak	चेतक	a famous horse
Chetan	चेतन	consciousness
Chetana	चेतना	consciousness
Chetananand	चेतनानन्द	supreme joy
Chhaya	छाया	shadow
Chhayank	छायांक	moon
Chidaakash	चिदाकाश	absolute Brahma
Chidatma	चिदात्मा	supreme spirit
Chidambar	चिदांबर	sky like heart
Chinmay	चिन्मय	the supreme being
Chintamani	चिन्तामणि	a fabulous gem
Chintak	चिन्तक	thinker
Chintan	चिन्तन	thinking
Chiranjeev	चिरंजीव	long lived
Chirantan	चिरन्तन	ancient

Chirantana	चिरन्तना	ancient (female)
Chiti	चिति	knowledge
Chitra	चित्रा	picture-like
Chitrangada	चित्रांगदा	Arjuna's wife (woman)
Chitrabhanu	चित्रभानु	the sun
Chitrada	चित्रदा	name of Arjun's wife
Chitragupt	चित्रगुप्त	god of destiny
Chitrakanta	चित्रकान्ता	an ancient name
Chitraketu	चित्रकेतु	with beautiful banner
Chitrakta	चित्राक्ता	hearenly voice (woman)
Chitralekha	चित्रलेखा	artist (female)
Chitra-netra	चित्रानेत्र	excellent eyed person
Chitraranjan	चितरंजन	who pleases the mind
Chitra-sen	चित्रसेन	artist
Chitra-vasu	चित्रवसु	shining star
Chitr-Baahu	चित्रबाहु	with beautiful hands
Chitswaroop	चितस्वरूप	the supreme spirit
Choksh	चोक्ष	pure and clean
Chooda-mani	चूड़ामणि	a jewel
Chushini	चुशिनी	brilliant
Chyavan	च्यवन	name of a saint

D द, ध

Daamini	दामिनी	lightning
Daamodar	दामोदर	a name of Krishna
Daaruk	दारुक	charioteer of Krishna, a tree
Daarun	दारुण	hard
Dadhichi	दधीचि	name of a saint
Devat	देवत	related to god
Daksh	दक्ष	a son of Brahma, capable
Daksha	दक्षा	capable, efficient (female)
Dakshata	दक्षता	daughter of art
Dakshesh	दक्षेश	name of lord Shiva
Dakshina	दक्षिणा	southward, incarnation of goddess Lakshmi
Dalpati	दलपति	commander of group
Damayanti	दमयन्ती	wife of King Nal
Dandak	दण्डक	a forest
Dandapani	दण्डपणि	an epithet for yoma
Danu	दनु	wife of Kashyap
Darpan	दर्पण	mirror
Darshak	दर्शक	spectator
Darshan	दर्शन	vision
Darshana	दर्शना	one who looks beautiful (female)

Darshita	दर्शिता	displayed
Dashrath	दशरथ	father of Rama, one who has 10 chariots
Datta	दत्त, दत्ता	one who is given
Daya	दया	mercy
Dayal	दयाल	kind hearted
Dayamay	दयामय	full of mercy
Dayanand	दयानन्द	one who enjoys being merciful, founder of Arya Samaj
Dayanidhi	दयानिधि	treasure of kindness
Deeksha	दीक्षा	initiation
Deenadayal	दीनदयाल	humble and merciful
Deena-Nath	दीनानाथ	lord of the poor
Deepa	दीपा	a shining woman
Deepali	दीपाली	a row of lights
Deepak	दीपक	light, candle
Deepankar	दीपंकर	one who lights the lamp
Deependra	दीपेन्द्र	Lord of the lights
Deepika	दीपिका	one who shows the way
Deepti	दीप्ति	a shining woman
Dev Vrata	देवव्रत	name of ancient King
Dev	देव	god
Devangana	देवांगना	goddess
Devapi	देवापि	an ancient King
Devadatt	देवदत्त	gift of the God

Devagya	देवज्ञ, देवज्ञा	with knowledge of God
Devahuti	देवाहूति	sacrifice to God
Devaki	देवकी	mother of lord Krishna
Devakinandan	देवकीनन्दन	name of Lord Krishna
Devakumari	देवकुमारी	daughter of a God
Devakumar	देवकुमार	son of a God
Deval	देवल	name of a saint
Devala	देवला	a famous ancient woman
Devalakshmi	देवलक्ष्मी	wealth of the god
Devanand	देवानन्द	joy of god
Devashri	देवश्री	fate, fortune
Devdas	देवदास	servant of the Lord
Devdas	देवदास	slave of god
Devidas	देवीदास	servant of the god
Devendra	देवेन्द्र	king of gods
Devendranath	देवेन्द्रनाथ	lord of gods
Devi	देवी	a female deity, goddess
Devika	देविका	divine
Devilal	देवीलाल	son of goddess
Devraaj	देवराज	king among gods, name of Indra
Devsena	देवसेना	army of god
Devta	देवता	saint
Dev-Vrat	देवव्रत	one who has taken a religious vow
Devyani	देवयानी	daughter of lord Shankar

Dhaara	धारा	a stream of water
Dhaarna	धारणा	view, notion
Dhaarini	धारिणी	the earth
Dhatri	धात्री	foster-mother, the earth
Dhanada	धनदा	one who gifts wealth
Dhanalakshmi	धनलक्ष्मी	goddess of wealth
Dhananjay	धनंजय	name of Arjuna, one who wins wealth
Dhanapati	धनपति	lord of wealth
Dhanesh	धनेश	lord of wealth
Dhaneshwari	धनेश्वरी	goddess of wealth (female)
Dhanishth	धनिष्ठ	devotee of wealth
Dhanvantari	धनवन्तरि	the physician of the God
Dhara	धरा	the earth
Dharam-nishth	धर्मनिष्ठ	one who has faith in religion
Dharitri	धरित्री	the earth
Dharma	धर्म, धर्मा	religion
Dharmadas	धर्मदास	servant of religion
Dharmadev	धर्मदेव	lord of religion
Dharmakirti	धर्मकीर्ति	fame of religion
Dharmaketu	धर्मकेतु	one who flies religious flag
Dharmaraj	धर्मराज	king of religion
Dharmaveer	धर्मवीर	protector of religion
Dharmendra	धर्मेन्द्र	master of religion
Dharmesh	धर्मेश	master of religion

Dharm-Mitra	धर्ममित्र	friend of religion
Dharmpaal	धर्मपाल	protector of religion
Dhaumya	धौम्य	a famous saint
Dhaval	धवल	white
Dhavala	धवला	fair complexioned (woman)
Dheeraj	धीरज	patience, consolation
Dheerandra	धीरेन्द्र	lord of the brave
Dhriti	धृति	the earth, firmness
Dhruv	ध्रुव	the polar star
Dhyaneshwar	धयानेश्वर	master of meditation
Digambar	दिगम्बर	naked
Digant	दिगन्त	end of the horizon
Digvijay	दिग्विजय	conquest of all directions
Dileep	दिलीप	a king of solar race
Dinakar	दिनकर	the sun
Dinendra	दिनेन्द्र	lord of the day, the sun
Dinesh	दिनेश	the sun
Divaakar	दिवाकर	the sun
Divya	दिव्या	divine (female), brilliant
Divyamoorti	दिव्यमूर्ति	a radiant idol
Divyangana	दिव्यांगना	one who has a radiant body
Drashta	द्रष्टा	one who sees
Draupadi	द्रौपदी	wife of Pandavas
Drishti	दृष्टि	vision

Dron	द्रोण	sacred wooden utencil, prominent Mahabharat character
Drupad	द्रुपद	father of Draupadi
Dugdha	दुग्धा	pure like milk (female)
Duhita	दुहिता	daughter, girl
Durga	दुर्गा	goddess of bravery
Durgesh	दुर्गेश	lord of forts
Durjay	दुर्जय	unconquerable
Durlabh	दुर्लभ	rare
Durvasa	दुर्वासा	ill clothed, a saint
Dushkrit	दुष्कृत	sinner
Dushyant	दुष्यन्त	name of a King
Dwaarka	द्वारका	capital of Shri Krishna's Kingdom
Dwaarka-Das	द्वारकादास	servant of Dwaarka
Dwaarka-Nath	द्वारकानाथ	lord of Dwaarka
Dweep	द्वीप	island
Dyuti	द्युति	brightness (female)

E ए

Ekagra	एकाग्र	concentration
Ekakini	एकाकिनी	loneliness
Ekaaksh	एकाक्ष	one eyed, Shiva
Ekaant	एकान्त	solitary
Ekaatma	एकात्मा	oneself, alone
Ekalavya	एकलव्य	a pupil of Guru Dronachaarya
Ekaling	एकलिंग	name of lord Shiva
Ekata	एकता	unity
Ek-dant	एकदन्त	another name of Ganesha
Ek-deo	एकदेव	supreme
Ekendra	एकेन्द्र	one god
Ek-jyoti	एक ज्योति	sole light
Ek-Nath	एकनाथ	name of a saint
Ekodar	एकोदर	brother
Ekodara	एकोदरा	sister
Ela	एला	cardamum, elaichi
Enakshi	एनाक्षी	beautiful eyes
Esha	एषा	desire
Eshana	एषणा	desire

F फ

Falgun	फाल्गुन	name of a Hindi month
Falguni	फाल्गुनी	day of full moon
Falagam	फलागम	producer of fruit
Falak	फलक	sky
Falgu	फल्गु	name of a river
Fani	फणी	serpent
Faneeshwar	फणीश्वर	king of serpents, Shiva
Faneendra	फणीन्द्र	king of serpent, Shiva

✧ ✧ ✧

G ग, घ

Gandhaari	गांधारी	wife of Dhritarashtra
Gaargi	गार्गी	wife of saint Yagyavalkya
Gaatha	गाथा	story
Gayatri	गायत्री	a sacred verse of Hindus
Gadadhar	गदाधर	name of lord Vishnu
Gagan	गगन	sky
Gaganavihari	गगनविहारी	wanderer in the sky
Gaganpriya	गगनप्रिया	beloved of sky
Gajanan	गजानन	like elephant eyes
Gajadhar	गजाधर	who can command an elephant
Gajbaahu	गजबाहु	who has strength of an elephant
Gajdant	गजदन्त	elephant teeth, Ganesha
Gajendra	गजेन्द्र	lord of the elephants, Ganesha
Gaj-gamini	गजगामिनी	lady who walks gracefully like elephant
Gajkaran	गजकर्ण	ears of elephant
Gajlakshmi	गजलक्ष्मी	goddess Lakshmi
Gajpati	गजपति	master of elephant, Ganesha
Gajvadan	गजवदन	name of lord Ganesha

Gambheer	गम्भीर	deep, sereious
Gambheera	गम्भीरा	serious (female)
Ganak	गणक	an astrologer
Ganapati	गणपति	name of lord Ganesha
Gandha	गंधा	a sweet smelling
Gandharv	गंधर्व	master in music
Ganesh	गणेश	son of lord Shiva
Ganga	गंगा	most sacred Indian river
Gangadatt	गगादत्त	gift of river Ganges
Gangadhar	गंगाधर	name of lord Shiva
Gangey	गांगेय	name of Bheeshma
Gangotri	गंगोत्री	origin of river Ganges
Ganika	गणिका	a dancer
Gan-Nath	गणनाथ	an epithet of Shiva
Garg	गर्ग	name of a saint, a caste
Garima	गरिमा	greatness, grace
Garjan	गर्जन	thunder
Garuda	गरुड़	the King of birds, falcon
Gati	गति	speed
Gaunrangi	गौरांगी	wife of Shiva, fair complexioned
Gaura	गौरा	name of Parvati (female)
Gauraang	गौरांग	fair complexioned, Shiva
Gaurishankar	गौरीशंकर	peak of the Himalayas
Gautam	गौतम	a saint, name of Buddha

Gaveshan	गवेषण	search
Gaveshana	गवेषणा	search (female)
Gaya	गया	a Buddhist pilgrim in India
Geeta	गीता	sacred Hindu book
Geeti	गीति	a song
Geetika	गीतिमा	a short song
Gehini	गेहिनी	house wife
Ghana-nand	घनानन्द	happy like clouds
Ghanashyam	घनश्याम	black clouds, Krishna
Giri	गिरि	mountain
Giridhar	गिरिधर	holder of mountains, name of Krishna
Girija	गिरिजा	name of Parvatee
Girilal	गिरिलाल	son of mountain
Giriraaj	गिरिराज	king of mountains
Girish	गिरीश	lord of mountains, Shiva
Girvaan	गिर्वाण	language of God
Gitanjali	गीतांजलि	handful of songs
Gobhil	गोभिल	a sanskrit scholar
Godavari	गोदावरी	name of a river
Gokul	गोकुल	a village near Mathura
Gomateshwar	गोमटेश्वर	sacred place for Jains
Gopaal	गोपाल	protector of cows, Krishna
Gopi	गोपी	protector of cows (female)
Gorakh-Nath	गोरखनाथ	saint of Gorakh community
Goswami	गोस्वामी	master of cows

Govardhan	गोवर्धन	name of a mountain
Govind	गोविन्द	name of Krishna
Greeshma	ग्रीष्म	summers
Gulaab	गुलाब	rose
Gulnaar	गुलनार	red flower
Gunaakar	गुनाकर	an ancient King
Gunesh	गुणेश	lord of qualities
Gunjan	गुंजन	sounding, echoing
Gunkiri	गुणकीरी	full of merits
Gun-nidhi	गुणनिधि	treasure house of virtues
Gun-ratna	गुणरत्ना	full of good qualities
Guru	गुरु	teacher, master
Gurubachan	गुरुबचन	voice of the Guru
Gurucharan	गुरुचरण	feet of the Guru
Gurudas	गुरुदास	servant of the Guru
Gurudatt	गुरुदत्त	gift of the Guru
Granthika	ग्रंथिका	narrator, intellectual lady
Gyanendra	ज्ञानेन्द्र	lord of knowledge

◇ ◇ ◇

H ह

Hakikat	हकीकत	reality
Hansa	हंस/हंसा	swan (male / female)
Hansgamini	हंस गामिनी	graceful woman
Hansraaj	हंसराज	king of swans
Hanuman	हनुमान	monkey god, deity of lord Rama
Har	हर	name of Shiva, forgiver of sins
Hareendra	हरीन्द्र	lord of Hari (krishna)
Hari Om	हरि ओम	name of Brahma
Hari Ram	हरि राम	name of god
Hari	हरि	name of Vishnu, green clour
Haribhajan	हरिभजन	hymns in praise of god
Haricharan	हरिचरण	feet of the lord
Haridaas	हरिदास	servant of Hari
Harihar	हरिहर	Shiva & Vishnu together
Harikrishan	हरिकृष्ण	Hari and Krishna together
Harinaakshi	हरिणाक्षी	having eyes like a deer
Harindranath	हरीन्द्रनाथ	lord of Hari
Harini	हरिणी	female deer (woman)
Haripriya	हरिप्रिया	beloved of Hari
Harishchandra	हरिश्चन्द्र	a legendary king
Harit	हरित	green
Harivansh	हरिवंश	family of Hari
Harivilaas	हरिविलास	the pleasure of Hari
Harsha	हर्ष/हर्षा	joy
Harshad	हर्षद	one who showers joy
Harshavardhan	हर्षवर्धन	one who enhances delight

Heera	हीरा	diamond
Hema	हेम/हेमा	gold
Hemaadri	हेमाद्रि	mountain of gold
Hema-Malini	हेमामालिनी	garland of gold
Hemant	हेमन्त	name of a season
Hemanti	हेमन्ती	who shines like gold (female)
Hema-Vati	हेमावती	name of Parvati
Hem-Chander	हेमचन्द्र	golden moon
Hemendra	हेमेन्द्र	lord of gold
Hemlata	हेमलता	golden creeper
Hemraaj	हेमराज	king of gold
Hima	हिम/हिमा	snow
Himadri	हिमाद्रि	snow mountain
Himanshu	हिमांषु	cold (ice) rays
Himachal	हिमाचल	the Himalaya's
Hina	हिना	a fragrance, mehndi
Hiranya	हिरण्य	a precious metal
Hiranyaaksh	हिरण्याक्ष	a demon
Hiranyamay	हिरण्यमय	golden
Hiranyamayi	हिरण्यमयी	golden (female)
Hiresh	हीरेश	king of gems
Hitarthi	हितार्थी	a well wisher
Holika	होलिका	colourful (female)
Hriday	हृदय	the heart
Hridaynath	हृदयनाथ	lord of the heart
Hridayesh	हृदयेश	lord of the heart
Hrishikesh	हृषिकेश	an epithet of Vishnu
Huma	हुमा	bird of panore

✧ ✧ ✧

इ, ई

Ichha	इच्छा	desire, wish
Iha	ईहा	desire
Ijya	इज्या	an image, a gift
Ikshin	ईक्षिन	eyes
Ikshu	इक्षु	sugarcane
Ikshuda	इक्षुदा	sweet tongue
Ikshu-malini	इक्षुमालिनी	name of a river
Ikshwaku	इक्ष्वाकु	ancestor of solar King
Ila	इला	the earth, name of Parvati
Ilakshi	इलाक्षी	center of earth
Indivar	इंदीवर	the blue lotus
Indira	इंदिरा	wife of Vishnu, Lakshmi
Indra	इन्द्र	the god of Rain
Indraani	इन्द्राणी	wife of Indra
Indrarjun	इन्द्रार्जुन	bright and brave Indra
Indradatt	इन्द्रदत्त	gift of Indra
Indradyuman	इन्द्रद्युम्न	splendour of Indra
Indraneel	इन्द्रनील	an emerald
Indra-priya	इन्द्राप्रिय	blue lotus, goddes of wealth, Laksmi
Indrasen	इन्द्रसेन	eldest of the Pandavas
Indrasena	इन्द्रसेना	army of Indra

Indu	इन्दु	moon, camphor
Induja	इन्दुजा	daughter of moon
Indukant	इन्दुकान्त	moon stone
Indulekha	इन्दुलेखा	crest of the moon
Indumati	इन्दुमती	full moon (female)
Ingita	इंगिता	movements of a dance (female)
Ipsa	इप्सा	desire
Ipsit	इप्सित	desired
Ira	इरा	the earth
Iraavati	इरावती	name of a river
Irma	इर्मा	the sun
Ish	ईश	ruler, lord
Isha	ईषा	another name of Durga (female)
Ishan	ईषसण	the sun
Ishit	इषित	one who desires to rule
Ishita	इषिता	great achievement(female)
Ishm	ईष्म	cupid
Ishtak	ईष्टक	reverenced
Ishwar	ईश्वर	the supreme God
Ishwar-geet	ईश्वर गीत	song of God
Ishya	इष्या	spring season

J ज

Jagriti	जागृति	awakening
Jaahnavi	जाह्नवी	river Ganges
Janakidas	जानकीदास	servant of Jaanaki
Jaanakiraman	जानकीरमण	husband of Jaanaki
Jaanaki	जानकी	daughter of Janak, Sita
Jag Jeevan	जगजीवन	life of the world
Jagadamba	जगदम्बा	mother of the world, Durga
Jagadeep	जगदीप	light of the world
Jagadeesh	जगदीश	lord of the world
Jagadev	जगदेव	lord of the world
Jagamohan	जगमोहन	one who attracts the world
Jagan-naath	जगन नाथ	lord of the universe
Jagannaath	जगन्नाथ	lord of the world
Jagati	जगती	the earth
Jagchandra	जगचन्द्र	Moon of the universe
Jagjeet	जगजीत	conqueror of the world
Jahnavi	जाह्नवी	epithet of sacred river Gangs
Jai	जय	victory
Jaimini	जैमिनि	an ancient philosopher
Jaladhi	जलधि	ocean

Jalaj	जलज	lotus
Jalbaala	जलबाला	daughter of the water
Jaldhar	जलधर	clouds
Jamuna	जमुना	river Yamuna
Janaardan	जनार्दन	name of Vishnu
Janak	जनक	father, a king
Janamejay	जनमेजय	an ancient King
Janani	जननी	mother
Janpriya	जनप्रिय	beloved of the people
Jasaraaj	जसराज	King of fame
Jasveer	जसवीर	hero of fame
Jaswant	जसवन्त	victorious
Jataayu	जटायु	a semi-divine bird from Ramayana
Jawahar	जवाहर	jewel
Jaya	जया	name of Durga, victor (female)
Jayabala	जयबाला	daughter of victory
Jayachand	जयचन्द	ancient King of Kannauj
Jayadeep	जयदीप	light of victory
Jayadev	जयदेव	god of victory
Jayaditya	जयादित्य	victorious sun
Jayakrishan	जयकृष्ण	victorious Krishna
Jayalakshmi	जयलक्ष्मी	victorious Lakhsmi
Jayant	जयन्त	son of Indra
Jayanti	जयन्ती	name of Durga (female)

Jayashri	जयश्री	name of Lakshmi
Jeevan	जीवन	life
Jeevraaj	जीवराज	lord of life
Jhankaar	झंकार	murmuring sound
Jigyasu	जिज्ञासु	thirst of knowledge
Jinabhadra	जिनभद्र	a Jain saint
Jinendra	जिनेन्द्र	lord of life
Jitendra	जितेन्द्र	lord of conquerors
Juhi	जूही	a flower
Jwaala	ज्वाला	flame
Jwalant	ज्वलन्त	flaming
Jyoti	ज्योति	flame
Jyotika	ज्योतिका	a Kind of flower
Jyotindra	ज्योतिन्द्र	lord of life
Jyotirmay	ज्योतिर्मय	starry
Jyotish	ज्योतिष	astrology
Jyotishmati	ज्योतिष्मती	luminous night
Jyotsna	ज्योत्स्ना	light of the moon

◇ ◇ ◇

K क, ख

Kadambari	कादम्बरी	the moon
Kaajal	काजल	lamp black, an eye cosmetic
Kaakali	काकली	sweet tone
Kaalidaas	कालीदास	servant of Goddess Kali
Kaali	काली	name of Durga
Kaalicharan	काली चरण	devotee of goddess Kali
Kaalika	कालिका	name of goddes Durga
Kaalindi	कालिन्दी	river Yamuna
Kaaliya	कालिया	a huge serpent
Kaamakshi	कामाक्षी	woman having voluptuous eyes
Kaam-Dev	कामदेव	god of love and passions
Kaamini	कामिनी	full of desires
Kaamyak	काम्यक	an ancient forest
Kaanan	कानन	forest, name of young Krishna
Kanksha	कांक्षा	desire
Kaanta	कान्ता	beloved, lovely
Kaanti	कान्ति	lustre
Kaarika	कारिका	actress
Kaartik	कार्तिक	name of a Hindi month

Kaartikey	कार्तिकेय	son of Shiva
Kaashi	काशी	name of sacred city Varanasi
Kaashinath	काशीनाथ	lord of Kashi, sacred city Varansi
Katyayan	कात्यायन	name of an ancient grammarian
Kaatyayani	कात्यायनी	another name of Parvatl
Kaaveri	कावेरी	name of a river
Kabeer	कबीर	faith, a sufi saint
Kadali	कदली	banana, lucky fruit(female)
Kadamb	कदम्ब	name of a tree
Kadambini	कादम्बिनी	garland of clouds (female)
Kaikeyi	कैकेयी	step mother of Lord Rama
Kailash	कैलाश	a mountain, sacred to Hindus
Kaivalya	कैवल्य	perfect isolation
Kala	कला	art (female)
Kalavati	कलावती	one who embodied art
Kalicharan	कालीचरण	feet of goddess Kaalee
Kal-hans	कलहंस	swan
Kaling	कलिंग	a bird
Kallol	कल्लोल	joy
Kallolini	कल्लोलिनी	who is always happy (female)
Kalpana	कल्पना	imagination (female)
Kalpita	कल्पिता	imagined (female)
Kalyaan	कल्याण	welfare
Kalyaani	कल्याणी	an auspicious woman

Kamal	कमल	lotus
Kamala	कमला	epithet of Lakshmi(female)
Kamalapati	कमलापति	name of lord Vishnu
Kamal-nayan	कमलनयन	lotus eyed
Kamalesh	कमलेश	lord of lotus
Kamalini	कमलिनी	a lotus plant (female)
Kanak	कनक	gold
Kanak-lata	कनकलता	a golden creeper (female)
Kanak-Prabha	कनकप्रभा	splender of gold (female)
Kanchan	कंचन	gold
Kandarp	कंदर्प	God of love
Kanika	कणिका	a small fragment (female)
Kanishk	कनिष्क	an ancient King
Kankan	कंकण	an ornament
Kanav	कणव	name of a saint
Kanya	कन्या	daughter
Kapil	कपिल	fair coloured
Kapila	कपिला	fair complexioned (female)
Kapildev	कपिलदेव	master of Kapil
Karmendra	कर्मेंद्र	duty performer
Karn	कर्ण	ear, a character of Mahabharata
Karnika	कर्णिका	bud, heart of lotus (female)
Karpoor	कर्पूर	camphor
Karuna	करुणा	tenderness, compassion
Karunanidhi	करुणानिधि	treasure of compassion
Kashyap	कश्यप	name of a saint musk
Kastoori	कस्तूरी	musk

Kaumudi	कौमुदी	moon light
Kaushal	कौशल	clever
Kaushalya	कौशल्या	mother of Rama
Kaushik	कौशिक	an epithet of Vishwamitra
Kaushiki	कौशिकी	goddess Durga
Kaustubh	कौस्तुभ	a precious stone
Kautilya	कौटिल्य	name of Chanakya
Kavi	कवि	poet
Kavita	कविता	poetry (female)
Kedaar	केदार	mountain, meadow
Keertan	कीर्तन	songs of worship
Keerti	कीर्ति	fame
Keka	केका	cry of peacock
Kesar	केसर	saffron
Kesari	केसरी	saffron coloured
Keshav	केशव	name of Krishna
Keshini	केशनी	woman with long hair
Ketaki	केतकी	a flower
Ketan	केतन	pure gold, house
Khagendra	खगेन्द्र	lord of the birds
Khyaati	ख्याति	fame
Kiraat	किरात	hunter, spreaking
Kiran	किरण	ray, beam
Kirit	किरिट	crown, shining
Kishor	किशोर	a young boy
Kishori	किशोरी	a young girl
Kokila	कोकिला	cuckoo, sweet singer
Komal	कोमल	tender, delicate
Kraanti	क्रान्ति	revolution

Kripa	कृपा	mercy
Krishan	कृष्ण	black, lord Krishna
Krishna	कृष्णा	name of a river, lord Krishna
Kriti	कृति	a composition
Kritika	कृतिका	the third lunar
Kshama	क्षमा	forgiveness
Kshema	क्षेमा	a prosperous woman
Kshemendra	क्षेमेन्द्र	lord of welfare
Kshipra	क्षिप्रा	fast, swift (female)
Kshiti	क्षिति	the earth
Kshitij	क्षितिज	horizon
Kuber	कुबेर	god of riches
Kulbhushan	कुलभूषण	one who brings honour to family
Kumaar	कुमार	young boy
Kumaari	कुमारी	the virgin (female)
Kumaaril	कुमारिल	a learned scholar
Kumud	कुमुद	white lotus
Kumudini	कुमुदिनी	a water lily
Kunaal	कुणाल	son of king Ashoka, a bird
Kundalini	कुण्डलिनी	an epithet of Varuna
Kundan	कुन्दन	pure gold
Kuntal	कुन्तल	lock of hair
Kunti	कुन्ती	mother of the Pandavas
Kusum	कुसुम	flower
Kusumita	कुसुमिता	filled with flower

L ल

Laalsa	लालसा	extreme desire
Laavanya	लावण्य	beauty
Laghav	लाघव	swiftness
Lajamayi	लज्जमयी	filled with bashfulness
Lajja	लज्जा	bashfulness, shame
Laksh	लक्ष	aim, target
Lakshman	लक्ष्मण	brother of lord Rama
Lakshamikant	लक्ष्मीकान्त	Vishnu, husband of goddess Lakshmi
Lakshami	लक्ष्मी	Goddess of wealth
Lakshmi-pati	लक्ष्मीपति	another name of Vishnu
Lalna	ललना	a young woman
Lalit Mohan	ललित मोहन	name of lord krishna, attractive
Lalit	ललित	lovely, fine
Lalita	ललिता	a lovely woman
Lata	लता	creeper
Latika	लतिका	a small creeper
Lav	लव	son of lord Rama, fragment
Lavalina	लवलीना	small, lovely
Lavangi	लवंगी	with fragmented body
Leela	लीला	beautiful woman

Leelavati	लीलावती	charming
Leena	लीना	intimately engrossed, devoted
Lekha	लेखा	account, calculation
Lochana	लोचना	woman with beautiful eyes
Lokankar	लोकांकर	creator of the world
Lokadhipati	लोकाधिपति	master of the world
Loka-kriti	लोकाकृति	creator of all the worlds
Lokesh	लोकेश	lord of the world
Lokgeet	लोकगीत	conquerer of the world, folk song
Lokita	लोकिता	beheld, viewed
Loknath	लोकनाथ	lord of the world
Lok-paal	लोकपाल	protector of the world
Loma	लोमा	with long hair
Lopa	लोपा	disappeared, vanished (female)

M म

Madhav	माधव	another name of Krishna
Madhavi	माधवी	another name of Lakshmi
Madhuri	माधुरी	sweetness
Magadhi	मागधी	name of daughter of Magadh king
Maagh	माघ	name of a Hindu month
Maala	माला	a garland
Malavika	मालविका	with of garland
Maalini	मालिनी	a female florist
Maalti	मालती	a flower plant
Maanas	मानस	born from the mind, intelligent
Maanasi	मानसी	goddess of learning
Manavendra	मानवेन्द्र	king, great men
Mandavi	माण्डवी	name of the wife of Bharata
Mandhata	मान्धाता	an ancient King
Maanik	माणिक	ruby, a stone
Manini	मानिनी	a proud woman
Markandeya	मार्कण्डेय	name of a saint
Martand	मार्तण्ड	the sun
Maruti	मारुति	another name of Hanumaan
Maya	माया	illusion

Madaalsa	मदालसा	name of a Goddess
Madan	मदन	god of love
Madan-manjari	मदनमंजरी	a sprout of love
Madan-mohan	मदन मोहन	attractive and lovable, name of Krishna
Madhulika	मधुलिका	sweet like honey
Madhu	मधु	honey
Madhubala	मधुबाला	a sweet woman
Madhukar	मधुकर	a bee, lover
Madhumalti	मधुमालती	sweet creeper
Madhumati	मधुमती	a sweet woman
Madhumeeta	मधुमीता	a sweet woman
Madhup	मधुप	a bee
Madhura	मधुरा	a sweet woman
Madhurima	माधुरिमा	sweetness (female)
Madhu-shala	मधुशाला	place of drinking
Madhusudan	मधुसूदन	another name of lord Krishna
Madhu-yamini	मधुयामिनी	sweet night
Madira	मदिरा	wine
Mahaakaali	महाकाली	an epithet of Durga
Mahaalakshmi	महालक्ष्मी	great goddess of wealth
Mahamaya	महामाया	an illusion, name of a diety
Mahashweta	महाश्वेता	an epithet of goddess saraswati
Mahaaveer	महावीर	most powerful
Mahabali	महाबली	strong

Mahadev	महादेव	another name of Shiva
Mahadevi	महादेवी	supreme deity (female)
Maharshi	महर्षि	a great saint
Maheepati	महीपति	the king
Mahesh	महेश	supreme god, name of Shiva
Maheshwar	महेश्वर	another name of Shiva
Maheshwari	महेश्वरी	another name of Durga
Maithili	मैथिली	another name of Sita
Maitrey	मैत्रेय	friendly
Maitreyi	मैत्रेयी	name of wife of saint Yagyavalkya
Maitri	मैत्री	friendship, daughter of Daksha
Makarand	मकरन्द	the honey of flower
Malay	मलय	a garden of Indra
Mallika	मल्लिका	a flower
Mamta	ममता	affection
Manmohan	मनमोहन	one who attracts the heart
Manan	मनन	thinking, thinker
Manaswi	मानस्वी	high minded
Manaswini	मानस्विनी	a high minded woman
Mandakini	मन्दाकिनी	another name of the Ganges
Mandaar	मन्दार	a flower, coral tree
Mandari	मन्दरी	a goddes, name of site (female)
Maneendra	मणीन्द्र	lord of gems

Maneesh	मनीश	lord of the mind
Maneesha	मनीशा	wisdom (female)
Maneeshi	मनीशी	wise
Manendra	मनेन्द्र	king of the mind
Mangal	मंगल	a planet
Mangala	मंगला	an auspicious woman
Mani	मणि	gem
Manikant	मणिकान्त	the blue jewel
Manimala	मणिमाला	a necklace of jewels
Manjari	मंजरी	sprout
Manju	मंजु	lovely
Manjul	मंजुल	handsome
Manjula	मंजुला	beautiful (female)
Manohar	मनोहर	one who wins over the mind
Manoj	मनोज	born of mind
Manorama	मनोरमा	who pleases the mind (female)
Manoranjan	मनोरंजन	entertainment
Manorath	मनोरथ	desire
Manu	मनु	the root of man, a sage
Maraal	मराल	swan
Mareechi	मरीचि	ray of light
Marut	मरुत	wind
Mathura	मथुरा	a religious city
Matsyendra	मत्स्येन्द्र	lord of fishes
Mayank	मंयक	moon

Mayukh	मयूख	brilliant, splendor
Mayur	मयूर	peacock
Mayuri	मयूरी	pea-hen
Medha	मेधा	intellect
Medhavi	मेधावी	wise
Medini	मेदिनी	earth
Meena	मीना	a kind of stone, enamel
Meenakshi	मीनाक्षी	fish eyed
Meera	मीरा	circumscribed, name of an ancient poetess
Meghana	मेघना	clouds
Meghashyam	मेघश्याम	black like a cloud
Megh-nad	मेघनाद	roar of clouds
Meha	मेहा	rain
Menaka	मेनका	name of an apsara, beautiful woman
Meru	मेरु	mountain
Mihir	मिहिर	the sun
Milan	मिलन	getting together
Milind	मिलिन्द	honey bee
Mithun	मिथुन	union
Mitra	मित्रा	a friend (woman)
Mohan	मोहन	fascinating, name of Lord Krishna
Mohini	मोहिनी	one who fascinates (female)
Mohit	मोहित	spell bound
Mohita	मोहिता	spell bond (female)

Moorti	मूर्ति	an idol
Moti	मोती	pearl
Mridani	मृदानी	an epithet of Parvatee
Mridul	मृदुल	tender, delicate
Mridula	मृदुला	delicate woman
Mriga	मृगा	a female deer (female)
Mrigendra	मृगेन्द्र	the lion
Mrig-Nayani	मृगनयनी	deer eyed woman
Mrinaal	मृणाल	lotus-stack
Mrityunjay	मृत्युन्जय	who has won over the death
Mudgal	मुद्गल	a saint
Mudit	मुदित	pleased
Mudita	मुदिता	a pleased woman
Mudra	मुद्रा	a seal, gesture of dance
Mudrika	मुद्रिका	a ring
Mugdha	मुग्धा	spell bound
Mukesh	मुकेश	an epithet for Shiva
Mukta	मुक्ता	a pearl
Mukti	मुक्ति	salvation, liberation
Mukul	मुकुल	a bud, blossom
Mukund	मुकुन्द	name of Vishnu
Muneendra	मुनीन्द्र	best among saints
Muraari	मुरारी	another name of lord Krishna
Murali	मुरली	the flute

❖ ❖ ❖

N न

Naabhi	नाभि	centre of body, name of an ancient King
Naag	नाग	a big serpent
Naagarjun	नागार्जुन	an ancient Philosopher
Naagbaala	नागबाला	daughter of the serpent
Naagendra	नागेन्द्र	king of the serpents
Naag-kanya	नागकन्या	daughter of the serpent
Naag-raj	नागराज	king of the serpents
Naam-dev	नामदेव	name of a saint
Nanak	नानक	first Sikh Guru
Narayan	नारायण	god, Lord Vishnu
Naarad	नारद	a celebrated ancient personality
Nabhit	नभित	fearless
Nav-jaat	नवजात	newly born
Nachiket	नचिकेत	fire
Nagendra	नगेन्द्र	lord of the mountains
Nahush	नहुष	name of an ancient King
Nakul	नकुल	brother of Sahdev
Nal	नल	an ancient King
Nalin	नलिन	lotus
Nalini	नलिनी	lotus (female)
Namita	नमिता	humble
Nand	नन्द	pleasure, father of Krishna

Nanda	नन्दा	prosperity
Nandan	नन्दन	son
Nandini	नन्दिनी	fabulous daughter
Nandita	नन्दिता	pleasant woman
Nand-Kishore	नन्दकिशोर	son of lord Krishna
Nandlal	नन्दलाल	son of Nand
Nand-Nandan	नन्दनन्दन	son of lord Krishna
Narasimha	नरसिंह	lion among men
Narendra	नरेन्द्र	king of human beings
Naresh	नरेश	lord of human beings
Narmada	नर्मदा	a holy river
Narottam	नरोत्तम	best among men
Natraaj	नटराज	king among actors, a Hindu symbol
Navaneet	नवनीत	fresh butter
Navin	नवीन	new
Nayan	नयन	eyes
Nayana	नयना	eyes (female)
Nayantaara	नयनतारा	eyes like stars
Neel	नील	blue
Neelanjana	नीलांजना	blue eyed
Neelam	नीलम	emerald
Neelima	नीलिमा	blue complexioned(female)
Neerad	नीरद	clouds
Neeraj	नीरज	a lotus
Neeraja	नीरजा	a lotus, a pearl (female)
Neerav	नीरव	quiet, silent
Neeti	नीति	moral, philosophy

Nidhi	निधि	treasure
Nihaar	नीहार	to see
Niharika	नीहारिका	heavy dew (female)
Niket	निकेत	house, mansion
Niketan	निकेतन	house, mansion
Nikhil	निखिल	entire
Nikunj	निकुंज	bower, arbor
Nilaya	निलय	house, mansion
Nimish	निमिष	twinkling, blinking
Niraala	निराला	exceptional
Niramay	निरामय	pure
Niramayi	निरामयी	pure woman
Nirmala	निर्मला	pure, without any dirt (female)
Niranjan	निरंजन	simple, Lord Shiva
Nirmal	निर्मल	pure, clear
Nirupama	निरुपमा	uncomparable
Nisha	निशा	night
Nishikant	निशिकान्त	the moon
Nishtha	निष्ठा	midnight honest (female)
Niteesh	नितीश	lord of law
Nitya	नित्य	eternal, native
Nitya	नित्या	constant (female)
Nivedita	निवेदिता	one who knows
Niyati	नियति	destiny
Noopur	नूपुर	ornaments of the feet
Nripendra	नृपेन्द्र	king of kings
Nutan	नूतन	novel, new

✧ ✧ ✧

O ओ

Odati	ओदती	sprinkling
Ojasvi	ओजस्वी	strong, brilliant
Ojaswini	ओजस्विनी	a very bright woman
Ojaswita	ओजस्विता	splendor, brilliance
Ojasya	ओजस्या	vigorous (female)
Ojati	ओजति	strong, with vital power
Ojishtha	ओजिष्ठा	best, powerful (female)
Om Prakash	ओम् प्रकाश	light of Om
Om	ओम्	sacred syllable/symbol used before Hindu prayers
Omesh	ओमेश	Lord of Om
Opash	ओपश	support, pillar
Omisha	ओमिशा	goddes of birth
Omkaar	ओंकार	mystic name for Hindu Gods, Sikh sacred symbol
Omkarnath	ओंकारनाथ	joy of syllable
Oshadhipati	ओषधिपति	lord of herbs
Oshadhi	ओषधि	herb, medicmi

✧ ✧ ✧

P प

Panchali	पांचाली	another name of Draupadi, wife of Pandavas
Paandu	पाण्डु	an ancient name, Pandavas
Paandurang	पाण्डुरंग	a diety
Paanini	पाणिनी	a Sanskrit grammarian
Parbrahm	पारब्रह्म	the supreme spirit
Parth	पार्थ	another name of Arjuna
Paarthiv	पार्थिव	earthly
Parvati	पार्वती	wife of lord Shiva
Paavak	पावक	pure
Paavan	पावन	pure, sacred
Paayal	पायल	anklet
Padm	पद्म	lotus
Padma	पद्मा	lotus, name of Lakshmi (female)
Padmakar	पद्माकर	the sun
Padmavati	पद्मावती	name of a river
Padmaja	पद्मजा	born out of lotus
Padmakanta	पद्मकान्ता	beautiful like lotus
Padma-lochan	पद्मलोचन	lotus eyed
Padm-greh	पद्मगृह	Lotus honsed, Goddes Lakshmi
Padmini	पद्मिनी	a lotus, a woman of beauty
Pallavi	पल्लवी	creeper in full bloom
Panchanan	पंचानन	five-eyed, name of Shiva

Pankaj	पंकज	name of lotus
Pankaja	पंकजा	flower born in mud(female)
Panna	पन्ना	emarald, a stone
Panit	पनित	praise, admiration
Paraag	पराग	pollen of sandal wood, celebrity
Parashar	पराशर	a celebrated saint
Parameshwar	परमेश्वर	the supreme God
Param-hans	परमहंस	the supreme spirit
Parashuraam	परशुराम	brave, an ancient sage
Paresh	परेश	supreme spirit
Parikshit	परीक्षित	an ancient king
Parimal	परिमल	perfume
Parimita	परिमिता	a moderate woman
Parjanya	पर्जन्य	rain
Parmarth	परमार्थ	highest truth, spiritual knowledge
Parna	पर्णा	leaves (female)
Parnika	पर्णिका	small plant (female)
Parvat	पर्वत	mountain
Pashupati	पशुपति	Lord of animals
Patanjali	पातंजलि	author of Sanskrit grammer
Pathik	पथिक	traveler
Paurav	पौरव	a descendent of King Puru
Pavan	पवन	wind
Pavitra	पवित्र	holy, sacred, pure
Payaswini	पयस्विनी	a milky cow
Peetambar	पीतांबर	yellow robed

Peeyush	पीयूज़	nectar
Phalgun	फाल्गुन	name of a Hindi month
Pinaki	पिनाकी	an epithet of Shiva
Pingal	पिंगल	a reputed sage
Pingala	पिंगला	another name of Lakshmee (female)
Pooja	पूजा	worship
Poonam	पूनम	night of full moon
Pooran	पूर्ण	complete
Poornanand	पूर्णानन्द	complete joy
Poornima	पूर्णिता	full moon night
Poorti	पूर्ति	fulfillment (female)
Poorv	पूर्व	the east
Poorvaj	पूर्वज	elder, ancestors
Poorvi	पूर्वी	eastern, ancient
Poosha	पूषा	a Vedic diety
Poshita	पोषिता	nourished
Prabha	प्रभा	splendor, radiance
Prabhaakar	प्रभाकर	the sun
Prashansa	प्रशंसा	praise
Prashant	प्रशान्त	very calm
Prasoon	प्रसून	flower
Prataap	प्रताप	glory, vigour
Prateechi	प्रतीची	westerly direction
Prateeksha	प्रतीक्षा	to wait, expectation
Pratibha	प्रतिभा	splendor, brilliance
Pratosh	प्रतोष	delight
Pratul	प्रतुल	a balanced person
Praveen	प्रवीण	expert, skilled

Prayaag	प्रयाग	name of holy city
Preetam	प्रीतम	lover
Preeti	प्रीति	love (female)
Preksha	प्रेक्षा	wise
Prem	प्रेम	love
Prerana	प्रेरणा	inspiration
Pritha	पृथा	another name of Kunti
Prithu	पृथु	broad
Prithvi	पृथ्वी	the earth
Pritish	प्रीतिश	lord of love
Priya	प्रिया	a favourite, beloved
Priyank	प्रियांक	very dear husband
Priyadarshi	प्रियदर्शी	good looking
Priyamvada	प्रियम्वदा	soft spoken
Priyanka	प्रियंका	with a beautiful mark
Puloma	पुलोमा	wife of Bhrigu
Puneet	पुनीत	pure
Puneeta	पुनीता	sacred (female)
Punya	पुण्या	a virtuous woman
Puru	पुरु	a legendary King
Purushottam	पुरुषोत्तम	best among men
Pushkar	पुष्कर	a blue lotus, pilgrim in Ajmer
Pushkarini	पुष्करिणी	a pond, female elephant
Push-Mitra	पुष्पमित्र	an ancient ruler
Pushp	पुष्प	flower
Pushpa	पुष्पा	a flower (female)
Pushpanjali	पुष्पांजलि	a floral tribute

✧ ✧ ✧

R र

Radha	राधा	prosperity, name of Krishna's wife
Radhika	राधिका	prosperity, wife of lord Krishna
Raja	राजा	king
Rajeev	राजीव	blue lotus
Rajeevlochan	राजीवालोचन	who has blue lotus eyes
Rajkumar	राजकुमार	prince
Rajsi	राजसी	passionate, name of goddess Durga
Rajyashri	राज्यश्री	propriety of a king
Raaka	राका	night full moon
Rakesh	राकेश	moon
Raakhi	राखी	a thread tied by sisters to brothers
Ram	राम	Lord Rama
Ramanuj	रामनुज	younger brother of Rama
Ram-Datt	रामदत्त	gift of Rama
Rameshwar	रामेश्वर	lord of Rama, a sacred bridge in south India
Ratri	रात्रि	night (female)
Rachana	रचना	creation, artistic work
Raghu	रघु	an ancient King of Avadh, speeding
Ragini	रागिनी	classical musical mode
Rahul	राहुल	name of Gautam Buddh's son
Rajani	रजनी	night
Rajeev	राजीव	blue lotus

Rajesh	राजेश	lord of Kings
Rajneesh	रजनीश	the moon, a modern philosopher
Raksha	रक्षा	protection
Rakshita	रक्षिता	protected
Rama	रमा	goddess Lakshmi
Ramakant	रमाकन्त	another name of Vishnu
Raman	रमण	pleasing
Ramani	रमणी	beautiful woman
Rambha	रम्भा	another name of Parvati, beautiful woman
Ramesh	रमेश	another name of Vishnu
Ramya	रम्या	pleasing
Ranjan	रंजन	pleasing
Ranjana	रंजना	pleasing (female)
Ranjeet	रंजीत	delighted coloured
Ran-veer	रणवीर	hero of the battle
Rashmi	रश्मि	ray
Rasik	रसिक	appreciator of beauty, tasteful
Rathin	रथिन	warrior
Rati	रति	daughter of Daksha, love
Ratna	रत्न	a precious stone
Ratnakar	रत्नाकर	the ocean
Ratnamala	रत्नमाला	a garland of gems
Ratnaprabha	रत्नप्रभा	luster of jewels
Raveendra	रवीन्द्र	the sun lord
Ravi	रवि	the sun
Ravikeerti	रविकीर्ति	famous like sun, renowned
Rekha	रेखा	a line
Renu	रेणु	dust, atom
Renuka	रेणुका	an ancient name
Reva	रेवा	name of a river

Revati	रेवती	prosperity
Richa	ऋचा	light, a vedic hymn
Riddhi	ऋद्धि	prosperity
Rijula	रिजुला	simple, honest
Rijuta	ऋजुता	sincerity
Rishabh	ऋषभ	morality
Rishi	ऋष्ज़ि	the saint
Rishikesh	ऋषिकेश	hair of a saint, a pilgrimage city
Riya	रिया	singer (female)
Ritambhara	ऋतम्भरा	goddess, the earth
Rituja	ऋतुजा	daughter of truth
Rituparna	ऋतुपर्णा	an ancient King
Rituraaj	ऋतुराज	king of weather
Rohini	रोहिणी	name of a star in Taurus
Rohit	रोहित	red horse of the sun
Roma	रोमा	a hairy woman
Roopa	रूपा	beautiful (female)
Roopak	रूपक	dramatic composition
Roopmanjari	रूपमंजरी	beautiful (female)
Ruchi	रुचि	beautiful, interest, taste
Ruchika	रुचिका	beautiful (female)
Ruchir	रुचिर	handsome
Rudra	रुद्र	fearsome, name of lord Shiva
Rudra	रुद्रा	God of storms, name of lord Shiva
Rudraani	रुद्राणी	name of Goddess Parvati
Rukmi	रुक्मि	an ancient name
Rukmini	रुक्मिणी	wife of lord Krishna
Rupaali	रूपाली	beautiful girl
Rupesh	रूपेश	lord of beauty

✧ ✧ ✧

S श, ष, स

Saadhana	साधना	worship
Saagar	सागर	ocean
Saaras	सारस	swan
Saarika	सारिका	a bird
Saavitri	सावित्री	a ray of light
Sabha	सभा	congregation
Sabhajit	सभाजित	honoured, praised
Sachidananda	सच्चिदानन्द	joy of the supreme
Sachit	सचित्	joy
Salil	सलिल	water
Saloni	सलोनी	beautiful
Samarpan	समर्पण	dedicating
Sambhooti	सम्भूति	birth, origin
Sameer	समीर	wind
Sampoorn	सम्पूर्ण	complete
Samriddhi	समृद्धि	prosperity
Sanatan	सनातन	permanent, everlasting
Sanchita	संचिता	collection (female)
Sandeep	संदीप	a lighted lamp
Sandhya	संध्या	evening
Sangeeta	संगीता	who knows to sing
Sangya	संज्ञा	awakening, knowledge

Sanjay	संजय	an ancient name in Mahabharat
Sanjeev	संजीव	one who lives happily
Sankalp	संकल्प	will, determination
Sannidhi	सन्निधि	proximity
Santosh	संतोज़	satisfaction
Sapana	सपना	dream
Saptarshi	सप्तर्ज़ि	seven stars representing seven great saints
Sarala	सरला	simple
Saras	सरस	juicy
Saraswati	सरस्वती	a diety, goddess of knowledge, name of a river
Sarita	सरिता	a river
Saroj	सरोज	lotus
Sarojini	सरोजिनी	cluster of lotus
Saryu	सरयू	name of a holy river
Sateendra	सतीन्द्र	lord of truth
Satya Bhama	सत्यभामा	wife of lord Krishna(female)
Satya	सत्य	truth
Satya	सत्या	truthfulness (female)
Satyajit	सत्यजित	victor of truth
Satyakaam	सत्यकाम	believer in truth
Satyashrawa	सत्यश्रवा	that who hears truth
Satyavaan	सत्यवान	truthful, an ancient king
Satyavati	सत्यवती	truthful (female)

Satyavrat	सत्यव्रत	strict in truth
Satyendra	सत्येन्द्र	lord of truth
Saubhadra	सौभद्र	gentle
Saubhagya	सौभाग्य	good luck
Saudamini	सौदामिनी	lightning
Saumitr	सौमित्र	good friend
Saumya	सौम्य	sober, serious
Saurabh	सौरभ	fragrance
Savita	सविता	the sun
Savya-Saachi	सव्यसाची	another name of Arjuna
Seema	सीमा	limit
Seeta	सीता	wife of lord Raama
Sena	सोनी	army
Seva	सेवा	service
Shakambhari	शाकम्भरी	a vegetable goddess
Shalini	शालिनी	housewife
Shaandilya	शांडिल्य	name of a saint
Shaanta	शान्ता	peaceful
Shaanti	शान्ति	peace
Sharada	शारदा	goddess of knowledge
Shardul	शार्दूल	a tiger
Shaashwat	शाश्वत	eternal
Shachi	शची	wife of God Indra
Shail	शैल	mountain
Shailaja	शैलजा	daughter of mountains

Shailendra	शैलेन्द्र	lord of the mountains
Shailesh	शैलेश	lord of the mountains
Shailesh	शैलेश	name of king of mountains
Shaivya	शैव्या	wife of king Harishchandra
Shakti	शक्ति	energy, strength
Shakuni	शकुनि	bird, uncle of Kauravas
Shakuntala	शकुन्तला	an ancient name
Shalaka	शलाका	thin stick
Shalya	शल्य	an arrow
Shama	शमा	candle (female)
Shambhu	शम्भु	another name of Shiva
Shankar	शंकर	another name of Shiva
Shankh	शंख	a shell
Shantanu	शान्तनु	peace-loving, father of Bhishma
Sharad	शरद	the autumn (season)
Sharatchandra	शरत्चन्द्र	moon of the autumn, a Bengali author
Sharadendu	शरदेन्दु	moon of autumn
Sharan	शरण	shelter
Sharada	शारदा	name of Saraswati(female)
Sharmila	शर्मिला	modest
Sharmishtha	शर्मिष्ठा	wife of king Yayaati
Sharvari	शर्वरी	night
Shashaank	शशांक	the moon
Shashi	शशि	the moon

Shashibala	शशिबाला	daughter of the moon
Shashikanta	शशिकान्ता	loved by moon (female)
Shashikala	शशिकला	beauty of the moon (female)
Shashiprabha	शशिप्रभा	light of the moon
Shashishekhar	शशिशेखर	moon-crested, name of Shiva
Shashwat	शाश्वत	eternal
Shaashwati	शाश्वती	the earth
Shastri	शास्त्री	educated
Shataaneek	शतानीक	another name of Ganesha
Shataavari	शतावरी	night
Shatayu	शतायु	hundred years old
Shatakshi	शताक्षी	hundred eyed
Shatjit	शतजित	conqueror of hundreds
Shat-Manyu	शतमन्यु	another name of Indra
Shat-Padm	शतपद्म	hundred petaled lotus
Shat-Roop	शतरूप	with hundred faces
Shaunak	शौनक	name of a great saint
Shri Kirti	श्रीकीर्ति	the glory
Shridevi	श्रीदेवी	goddess of wealth
Shreeharsh	श्रीहर्ष	god of happiness
Shreekant	श्रीकान्त	an epithet of Vishnu
Shree-priya	श्रीप्रिया	divine, lover
Shreelata	श्रीलता	beautiful
Shreeman	श्रीमान	a respectable person

Shrimati	श्रीमती	a respectable lady
Shriparna	श्रीपर्णा	lotus
Shripadi	श्रीपदी	jasmine flower
Shripushp	श्रीपुष्प	sacred flower
Shrirang	श्रीरंग	another name of Vishnu
Shriranjani	श्रीरंजनी	lovely lady
Shriya	श्रीया	prosperity (female)
Shreevallabh	श्रीवल्लभ	lord of Lakshmi
Shrey	श्रेय	good fortune
Shreyas	श्रेयस	auspicious
Shrut-keerti	श्रुतकीर्ति	renowned, reputed
Shruti	श्रुति	sense of hearing
Shubha	शुभा	lustre
Shubhangi	शुभांगी	with pleasant physique
Shubhada	शुभदा	giver of happiness
Shubhra	शुभ्रा	fair complexioned lady
Shuchi	शुचि	pure, bright
Shuchismita	शुचिस्मिता	beautiful, bright (female)
Shuchita	शुचिता	purity
Shuddhi	शुद्धि	purity, holiness
Shuk	शुक	a parrot
Shukla	शुक्ला	white
Shweta	श्वेता	a crystal, white
Shyaam	श्याम	black
Shyaama	श्यामा	night, black (female)

Shyaamaka	श्यामका	blacken, ancient name
Shyaamal	श्यामल	dark blue
Shyaamali	श्यामली	dark complexioned lady
Siddhaa	सिद्धा	perfected lady
Siddhaarth	सिद्धार्थ	name of Buddha, enlightenment
Siddheshwari	सिद्धेश्वरी	successful, perfect lady
Siddhi	सिद्धि	perfection
Sindhu	सिन्धु	the sea
Sindhuja	सिन्धुजा	born of ocean
Sitanshu	सितांशु	the moon
Sitesh	सीतेश	lord of Sita
smaran	स्मरण	memory
Smita	स्मिता	smiling woman
Smriti	स्मृति	rememberance
Sneh	स्नेह	love, affection
Sneha	स्नेहा	an affectionate woman
Snehaprabha	स्नेह प्रभा	lustre of love
Snehlata	स्नेहलता	creeper of affection
Sohan	सोहन	good looking
Sohini	सोहिनी	pretty (female)
Som	सोम	moon, religious drink
Somendra	सोमेन्द्र	another name of Indra
Somnath	सोमनाथ	lord of the moon
Somsuta	सोमसुता	daughter of Soma

Sonaali	सोनाली	of gold
Sonal	सोनल	golden (female)
Sopaan	सोपान	stairs, steps
Spriha	स्पृहा	desire, eager (female)
Srotaswini	स्रोतस्विनी	a stream
Stuti	स्तुति	a song of prayer
Subaahu	सुबाहु	strong armed
Subandhu	सुबन्धु	a good friend
Subeer	सुबीर	courageous, braves
Subhalakshmi	सुभालक्ष्मी	radient, name of Lakshmi
Subhaagi	सुभागी	blessed
Subhaash	सुभाष	soft spoken
Subhashini	सुभाषिणी	sweet spoken (female)
Subhadra	सुभद्रा	an auspicious woman
Subhangi	सुभांगी	Beautiful, fair limbed
Subhaga	सुभागा	possesing good fortune (female)
Subodh	सुबोध	intelligent
Subodhini	सुबोधिनी	intelligent (female)
Subrahmanya	सुब्रह्मण्य	the god of war, Shiva
Sucharita	सुचरिता	of good character (female)
Sucheta	सुचेता	of fine mind (female)
Suchitra	सुचित्रा	good artise (female)
Sudaama	सुदामा	meek, humble, poor
Sudarshan	सुदर्शन	good looking

Sudarshini	सुदर्शिनी	good looking (female)
Sudeep	सुदीप	good looking
Sudeepta	सुदीप्त	beautiful (female)
Sudesh	सुदेश	good country
Sudev	सुदेव	good deity
Sudevi	सुदेवी	good woman
Sudha	सुधा	nectar (female)
Sudhaakar	सुधाकर	the moon
Sudhanshu	सुधांशु	the moon
Sudheer	सुधीर	resolute, patient
Sudheesh	सुधीश	lord of excellent intellect
Sugandh	सुगन्ध	sweet smelling, fragrance
Sugreev	सुग्रीव	with shapely neck
Suhaas	सुहास	with a lovely smile
Suhaasini	सुहासिनी	with lovely smile (female)
Sujaata	सुजाता	wellborn (female)
Sukanya	सुकन्या	gentle girl
Sukeerti	सुकीर्ति	good fame
Sukesh	सुकेश	with good hair
Sukesha	सुकेशा	with good hair (female)
Sukeshi	सुकेशी	with good hair (male)
Sukeshini	सुकेशिनी	with good hair (female)
Suketu	सुकेतु	of good banner, flag
Sukti	सुक्ति	beautiful verse (female)
Sukumaar	सुकुमार	very tender

Sulabha	सुलभा	easily obtainable
Sulakshana	सुलक्षणा	of good character
Sulalita	सुललिता	very tender (female)
Sulekha	सुलेखा	good composition (female)
Sulochana	सुलोचना	with beautiful eyes
Suman	सुमन	flower
Sumangal	सुमंगल	very auspicious
Sumangala	सुमंगला	very auspicious (female)
Sumati	सुमति	with good mind
Sumedha	सुमेधा	having good talent
Sumegha	सुमेघा	like beautiful clouds
Sumit	सुमित	beautiful cloud
Sumantra	सुमंत्रा	good hymn (female)
Sumitra	सुमित्रा	good friend
Sumukhi	सुमुखी	beautiful faced
Sunand	सुनन्द	pleasant
Sunandita	सुनन्दिता	delightful (female)
Sundar	सुन्दर	attractive, beautiful
Suneeta	सुनीता	good conduct (female)
Sunetra	सुनेत्रा	beautiful eyed (female)
Suparn	सुपर्ण	bird, ray of light
Suprabhaat	सुप्रभात	good morning
Suprasiddh	सुप्रसिद्ध	prominent, famous
Supriya	सुप्रिया	dearly, loved
Surabhi	सुरभि	sweet smelling

Suras	सुरस	juicy
Surati	सुरति	great enjoyment
Surbala	सुरबाला	daughter of music
Surdaas	सूरदास	servant of musical tunes, a famous Hindi poet
Surekha	सुरेखा	beautiful
Surendra	सुरेन्द्र	another name of Indra
Suresh	सुरेश	king of Gods
Suroopa	सुयपा	beautiful (female)
Suruchi	सुरुचि	good natured (female)
Surya	सूर्य	the sun
Suryabala	सूर्यबाला	daughter of the sun
Suryakant	सूर्यकान्त	loved by the sun
Sushant	सुशान्त	calm
Sushama	सुषमा	great lustre (female)
Susheel	सुशील	of good natured
Susheela	सुशीला	of good character (female)
Sushen	सुषेण	Vishnu son of Vasudeva
Sushrut	सुश्रुत	of good reputation
Swapn	स्वप्न	dream
Swapna	स्वप्ना	dream (female)
Swapnasundari	स्वप्न सुन्दरी	dream beauty (female)
Swarna	सवर्णा	golden beauty (female)
Swasti	स्वस्ति	greetings (female)
Swastika	स्वस्तिका	a lucky object (female)
Swayambhu	स्वयम्भू	self existent

◇ ◇ ◇

T त

Tamraparni	ताम्रपर्णी	copper like leafs
Taapasi	तापसी	a female ascetic
Taara	तारा	star
Tarak	तारक	saviour
Taarika	तारिका	a small star (female)
Takshak	तक्षक	a cobra
Talika	तालिका	nightingale
Tamas	तमस	darkness
Tameeshwar	तमीश्वर	lord of darkness, moon
Tandra	तन्द्रा	weariness
Tanuja	तनूजा	small daughter
Tanushri	तनुश्री	female with a divine body
Tanvi	तनवी	young
Tapan	तपन	hot season
Tapas	तपस	sun
Tapaswini	तपस्विनी	a female ascetic
Taralika	तरलिका	shaking
Taralita	तरलिता	diluting, strirred
Taramati	तारामती	loyal, wife of king Harishchandra
Tarang	तरंग	wave
Tarangini	तरंगिनी	river

Tarani	तरणी	rag of light (female)
Tarla	तरला	trembling, shaking
Tarulata	तरुलता	a creeper
Tarun	तरुण	young
Taruni	तरुणी	young woman
Tarunika	तरुणिका	young (female)
Teekshna	तीक्षणा	sharp witted (female)
Teerth	तीर्थ	holy place
Tejasi	तेजसी	energetic, brilliant
Tejaswini	तेजस्विनी	energetic, brilliant
Tejeshwar	तेजेश्वर	lord of brightness
Tejshri	तेजश्री	beauty of the lustre
Tilak	तिलक	ornamental mark on fore-head
Tilottama	तिलोत्तमा	name of an old beautiful woman
Titiksha	तितिक्षा	endurance
Toolika	तूलिका	brush
Toshita	तोषिता	a satisfied woman
Toyesh	तोयेष्ठ	lord of water
Triambak	त्र्याम्बक	another name of Shiva
Tribhuvan	त्रिभुवन	three world, heaven, hell and earth
Tribandh	त्रिबंधु	friend of three worlds
Trideep	त्रिदीप	consisting of three lights
Tridev	त्रिदेव	three gods in one

Trilochan	त्रिलोचन	three eyed
Trilochana	त्रिलोचना	three eyed (female)
Trilok	त्रिलोक	three worlds
Trilokesh	त्रिलोकेश	lord of three worlds
Tripti	त्रिप्ती	contented (female)
Tripan	त्रिपन	knowledge-full
Tripur	त्रिपुर	three cities
Tripurari	त्रिपुरारि	name of lord Shiva
Trishanku	त्रिशंकु	an ancient King
Trishita	तृषिता	thirsty (female)
Trishna	तृश्णा	thirst
Trishti	त्रिष्टि	satisfaction
Triveni	त्रिवेणी	where three rivers meet
Trividya	त्रिविद्या	learned
Trivikram	त्रिविक्रम	an epithet of Vishnu
Tuhin	तुहिन	snow
Tulsi	तुलसी	a plant with fragrance
Tulsidaas	तुलसीदास	servant of Tulsi, author of Ramayana
Tushar	तुषार	frost
Tushita	तुषिता	a deity (female)
Tushti	तुष्टि	satisfaction
Tyaagaraaj	त्यागराज	a deity

✧ ✧ ✧

U उ, ऊ

Uchatha	उचथा	delightful
Uchit	उचित	proper
Udadhi	उदधि	the sea
Uday	उदय	to rise
Udayagiri	उदयगिरी	eastern mountains
Uddhav	उद्धव	a friend of Krishna
Udgar	उदगर	joyous expressions
Udit	उदित	rising
Udyaan	उद्यान	garden
Ugra	उग्र	fierce
Ugrasen	उग्रसेन	an ancient King
Ujaas	उजास	light
Ujjwal	उज्ज्वल	bright
Ujjwalkeerti	उज्जवलकीर्ति	bright famed
Uksha	उक्षा	watery, strong
Ukti	उक्ति	speech
Ulka	उलका	a falling star
Ullaas	उल्लास	joy
Ullasini	उल्लासिनी	always cheerful
Uma	उमा	wife of Shiva
Umaakant	उमाकन्त	name of Shiva
Umapati	उमापति	name of Shiva

Umang	उमंग	enthusiasm
Umesh	उमेश	name of Shiva
Unmeelan	उन्मीलन	opening of eyes
Unmesh	उन्मेज़	opening
Unmesh	उन्मेश	visible
Unnati	उन्नति	progress
Upasana	उपासना	worship
Upaasya	उपास्य	worshippable
Upadesh	उपदेश	enlightenment, speech
Upamanyu	उपमन्यु	an ancient name
Upanishad	उपनिषद	Hindu scriptures
upantika	उपन्तिका	vicinity, neighbour
Upasana	उपासना	worship
Upendra	उपेन्द्र	another name of Vishnu
Upkaar	उपकार	obligation, beneficience
Urja	ऊर्जा	energy
Urjaswita	ऊर्जास्विता	powerful
Urmi	ऊर्मि	waves
Urmika	उर्मिका	high
Urjaswi	उर्जस्वी	energetice
Urmila	उर्मिला	sentimental
Urmya	उर्मया	night
Urna	उमा	light, splendour
Urva	उर्वा	a saint
Uruchaksha	उरुचक्षा	big eyed (female)

Urvashi	उर्वशी	name of a beautiful nymproh in Hindu mythology
Urvi	उर्वि	earth (female)
Urvija	उर्विजा	born of earth
Usha	ऊषा	dawn, early morning
Ushakiran	ऊषाकिरण	morning ray
Ushana	उषना	name of a saint
Ushma	ऊष्मा	warmth (female)
Ushna	ऊष्णा	hot tempered
Utkal	उत्कल	son of Dhruva
Utkarsh	उत्कर्ष	awakening, excellence
Utkrisht	उत्कृष्ट	best
Utpal	उत्पल	blue lotus
Utpala	उत्पला	blue lotus (female)
Utpalaakshi	उत्पलाक्षी	lotus eyed
Utsang	उत्संग	embrace
Utsarg	उत्सर्ग	dedicating
Utsuk	उत्सुक	anxious
Uttaanapaad	उत्तानपाद	father of Dhruva
Uttam	उत्तम	best
Uttama	उत्तमा	best (female)
Uttar	उत्तर	the north
Uttara	उत्तरा	wife of Abhimanyu(female)
Uttarayan	उत्तरायन	equator
Utthaan	उत्थान	to arise
Uttung	उत्तुंग	high

✧ ✧ ✧

V व

Vachaspati	वाचस्पति	lord of speech
vaachi	वाची	nector like speech of Goddes Lakshmi
Vageesh	वागीष	lord of speech
Vageshwari	वागेश्वरी	goddess of speech
Vakpati	वाक्पति	great orator
Valmeeki	वाल्मीकि	an ancient saint
Vaama	वामा	beautiful
Vaamakshi	वामाक्षी	beautiful eyed
Vaaman	वामन	name of Vishnu, dwarfish
Vaamdev	वामदेव	name of a Shiva
Vaangmati	वांगमती	name of a river
Vaangmayi	वांगमयी	literary
Vaani	वाणी	speech
Vaaridhi	वारिधि	ocean
Varija	वारिजा	lotus
Vaaruni	वारुणी	goddess
Vasavadatta	वासवदत्ता	a name in Sanskrit classics
Vasanti	वासन्ती	youthful, Jasmine
Vaasuki	वासुकी	a celestial cobra
Vatsyaayan	वात्स्यायन	a scholar of ancient times
Vaayu	वायु	wind

Vachan	वचन	promise
Vagdevi	वागदेवी	Goddess Saraswati, powerof speach
Vagmini	वाग्मिनी	skilful in speech
Vaibhav	वैभव	prosperity
Vaidarbhi	वैदर्भी	princes of Vidarbha
Vaidyanath	वैद्यनाथ	master of medicines, name of Shiva
Vaijayanti	वैजयन्ती	necklace of lord Vishnu
Vaijayantika	वैजयन्तिका	long necklace
Vaijayantimala	वैजयन्तीमाला	long necklace of fine jems
Vaikunth	वैकुण्ठ	heaven
Vaikunth-nath	वैकुण्ठनाथ	Vishnu, master of heavens
Vairochan	वैरोचन	an ancient name
Vaishaali	वैशाली	an ancient city
Vaishwanar	वैश्वानर	omnipresent
Vaitarani	वैतरणी	name of a river
Vaivaswati	वैवस्वती	name of Yamuna (female)
Vaiwaswat	वैवस्वत	one of the Manus (saints)
Vajrang	वजरंग	diamond bodied
Vajrabahu	वज्रबाहु	one with strong arms
Vajrapaani	वज्रपणि	holder of rocks
Vakratund	वक्रतुण्ड	an epithet of Ganesha
Vallabh	वल्लभ	beloved
Vallabhi	वल्लभी	beloved (female)

Vallari	वल्लरी	a creeper
Valli	वल्ली	a creeper (female)
Vanaja	वनजा	forest born
Vanashri	वनश्री	beauty of the forest
Vandan	वन्दन	adoration
Vandana	वन्दना	adoration, prayer
Vandaneeya	वन्दनीय	respectable
Vandaneeya	वन्दनीया	respectable (female)
Van-Devi	वनदेवी	goddess of jungle
Vandita	वन्दिता	praised
Vanita	वनिता	a woman
Vanlakshmi	वनलक्ष्मी	goddess of the forest
Vanlata	वनलता	forest creeper
Vanmaala	वनमाला	a garland from woods
Vanmaali	वनमाली	an epithet of Krishna, protector of woods
Van-raaj	वनराज	the lion
Vanshidhar	वंशीधर	flute player, Krishna
Vanshi	वंशी	flute
Vanshlakshmi	वंशलक्ष्मी	the fortune of the family
Vanya	वन्या	from the woods
Varaah	वराह	an epithet of Vishnu, pig
Varaahamihir	वराहमिहिर	an ancient astronomer
Varangana	वरांगना	a lovely woman
Varangi	वरांगी	with beautiful body

Varadaraaj	वरदराज	another name of Vishnu
Varanmaala	वर्णमाला	the alphabets
Varcha	वर्चा	energy
Varda	वरदा	a deity
Vardhman	वर्धमान	name of Vishnu, increasing
Varnika	वर्णिका	dress of an actor
Var-Prada	वरप्रदा	who grants blessings
Var-Ruchi	वररुचि	an ancient poet
Varsha	वर्षा	rains
Varshita	वर्षिता	rained
Vartanu	वरतनु	beautiful
Varun	वरुण	god of waters
Vasant	वसन्त	spring
Vasantamalika	वसन्तमालिका	garland of spring
Vasantika	वसन्तिका	yellow flower
Vasantlata	वसन्तलता	creeper of spring
Vasav	वसव	an epithet of Indra
Vashisht	वशिष्ट	name of a guru in Ramayana
Vasu	वसु	wealth, jewel
Vasudev	वसुदेव	father of Krishna, god of the universe
Vasudha	वसुधा	the earth
Vasumati	वसुमति	the earth
Vasumitr	वसुमित्र	an ancient name

Vasundhara	वसुन्धरा	the earth
Vasusen	वसुसेन	original name of king Karna
Vatsar	वत्सर	ultimate abode
Ved	वेद	divine knowledge, holy scriptures of Hindu
Vedaprakash	वेदप्रकाश	light of the Vedas
Vedika	वेदिका	small platform
Ved-Vyas	वेदव्यास	name of a saint
Veena	वीणा	musical instrument
Veer	वीर	powerful, brave
Veerbaala	बीवरबाला	courageous (female)
Veerendra	वीरेन्द्र	lord of courageous men
Vela	वेला	time
Veni	वेणी	braided hair
Venkatesh	वेंकटेश	name of God Vishnu
Venu	वेणु	bamboo, flute
Vetravati	वेत्रवती	name of a river
Vibha	विभा	night, glow
Vibhakar	विभाकर	the moon
Vibhavari	विभावरी	night
Vibhavasu	विभावसु	the sun
Vibhav	विभव	wealth, prosperity
Vibhooti	विभूति	majesty
Vibhu	विभु	powerful
Vidarbh	विदर्भ	ancient name of an Indian state

Videh	विदेह	without form
Vidhatri	विधातु	creator
Vidhu	विधु	the moon
Vidula	विदुला	an ancient name (female)
Vidur	विदुर	skilful
Vidushi	विदुशी	a scholar (female)
Vidya	विद्या	learning, education
Vidyaranya	विद्यारण्य	forest of learning
Vidyulata	विद्युल्लता	a streak of lightning
Vidyut	विद्युत	lightning, electricity
Vighneshwar	विधनेश्वर	lord of supreme knowledge
Vihangini	विहंगिनी	who flied like a bird
Vijay	विजय	victory
Vijaya	विजया	name of Durga, victor (female)
Vijayant	विजयन्त	victor, name of Indra
Vijaylakshmi	विजयलक्ष्मी	success of wealth
Vijigeesh	विजिगीष	desire of victory
Vikas	विकास	development
Vikasini	विकासिनी	development (female)
Vikram	विक्रम	valour
Vikrant	विक्रान्त	powerful
Vilaas	विलास	entertainment
Vilaasini	विलासिनी	entertainment (female)
Vilochan	विलोचन	the eye

Vimal	विमल	pure
Vimala	विमला	pure (female)
Vinayak	विनायक	remover of obstacles, Ganesha
Vinamra	विनम्र	humble
Vinata	विनता	humble (female)
Vinati	विनति	bowing down
Vinay	विनय	humbleness
Vinaya	विनया	humbleness (female)
Vindhyavasini	विन्ध्यवासिनी	who lives in forests
Vinita	विनीता	humble
Vinod	विनोद	joy, fun
Vinodini	विनोदिनी	fun loving (female)
Vipin	विपिन	forest garden
Viplav	विप्लव	revolution
Vipul	विपुल	extensive
Vipula	विपुला	the earth (female)
Viraaj	विराज	shining, name of saint Manu
Viraat	विराट	giant
Virachana	विरचना	arrangement
Viraja	विरजा	dustless
Viral	विरल	rare
Viranchi	विरांचि	name of Brahmaa
Viresh	वीरेश	lord of heroes
Virendra	वीरेन्द्र	God of braves

Virochan	विरोचन	shining
Vishaad	विशाद	spotless clean
Vishaakha	विशाखा	sixteen constellation
Vishaal	विशाल	broad
Vishaalaaksh	विशालाक्ष	large eyed
Vishaalaakshi	विशालाक्षी	broad eyed (female)
Vishikh	विशिख	arrow
Vaishnavi	वैष्णावी	name of a goddess
Vishnu	विष्णु	almighty
Vishnupriya	विष्णुप्रिया	another name of Tulasi
Vishram	विश्राम	relaxation
Vishudhi	विशुद्धि	pure
Vishv	विश्व	universe
Vishva-bandhu	विश्वबंधु	friend of the world
Vishvaketu	विश्वकेतु	an epithet of Aniruddh
Vishvam	विश्वम	universal
Vishvanaath	विश्वनाथ	lord of the universe
Vishvesh	विश्वेश	lord of the world
Vishwa	विश्वा	a holy river
Vishwaamitra	विश्वामित्र	friend of the world
Vishwaas	विश्वास	faith
Vishwajeet	विश्वजीत	conquerer of the world
Vishwakarma	विश्वकर्मा	architect of the universe
Vishwambhar	विश्वम्भर	the supreme spirit
Vishwaroop	विश्वरूप	omnipresent

Vishweshwar	विश्वेश्वर	lord of the universe
Vitasta	वितस्ता	name of a river
Vitthal	विट्ठल	a form of god Vishnu
Vivaswat	विवस्वत	the sun
Vivek	विवेक	reasoning, wisdom
Vivekini	विवेकिनी	judicious (female)
Viyogini	वियोगिनी	separated woman
Vrata	व्रता	firm (female)
Vriksha	वृक्ष	tree of Ashwatthama
Vrinda	वृन्दा	the holy basil
Vrishabh	वृषभ	religion
Vyaapti	व्याप्ति	universal pervasion
Vyom	व्योम	sky
Vyoma	व्योमा	sky (female)
Vyomang	व्योमांग	part of the sky
Vyomakesh	व्योमकेश	sky like hair
Vyomesh	व्योमेश	the sun
Vyomika	व्योमिका	who resides in sky
Vyomini	व्योमिनी	who lives in sky (female)

✧ ✧ ✧

Y य

Yaachana	याचना	a request
Yadav	यादव	a community
Yaadavi	यादवी	female member of Yadav community
Yagya-seni	याज्ञसेनी	another name of Draupadi
Yagyavalkya	याज्ञवल्क्य	name of a saint
Yaminee	यामिनी	night
Yadu	यदु	an ancient King
Yadunandan	यदुनन्दन	son of Yadu, Krishna
Yadupati	यदुपति	lord of Yadav community
Yagneshwar	यज्ञनेश्वर	lord of sacrifice
Yagya	यज्ञ	sacrifice, worship
Yagyasen	यज्ञसेन	name of king Drupad
Yagyesh	यज्ञेश	lord of the sacrificial fire
Yamee	यमी	sister of Yamuna
Yamuna	यमुना	name of a river
Yash	यश	fame
Yashodha	यशोदा	mother of Krishna
Yashodhan	यशोधन	rich in fame
Yashodhar	यशोधर	famous
Yashodhara	यशोधरा	wife of lord Buddha
Yashpal	यशपाल	who protects fame
Yati	यति	a saint

❖❖❖